AF449052

THE QPH METHOD: Change Your Beliefs, Thoughts & Emotions in 2 Minutes.

(Quick Guide Edition)

Contents

A New World: Your Secret to Success

You have a superpower inside of your own mind, that no one has revealed to you (*yet*).

What you will find in this book is written and hinted within the *Bible*, the *Quran* and many other religions & ancient scriptures.

This superpower is responsible for changing and controlling your life in ways that most people can't control. It's responsible for solving most personal and success-related problems for which we don't have real and complete solutions for.

It's your ability to **control** how you see the world - <u>the thoughts you think and the feelings you feel.</u> Predictably gaining control of the process.

If you experience any personal problem, success barrier, relationship issue or feel lack of purpose, you've picked up the right book.

This little book is not about solving a problem. It's about an ability which holds the power to solve most if not all of the problems you can ever encounter. And it's about solving them at the very root cause, <u>where they really get created.</u>

Back in 2016, one thing I wanted the most, I bounced back from my autoimmune disease and a life of hiding and living in bandages. But the problem I had was that my mindset that was created while I was sick - followed me.

Every time I looked around at people, creating relationships seemed natural to them. Where for me I was self-conscious, stressed and I still couldn't feel good in my own skin.

So, I picked up books on confidence in hopes to *'Improve'* my situation and build my confidence back up. I thought maybe I would find a tip, trick, a method that would help me bounce back – *that was all I needed.*

I've read over a 100 of books on confidence alone. Every time I tried something, it may have worked temporarily, from my belief that it does. But eventually I went back into the pit, and it was deeper than when I started off. The more I tried something, and it didn't work, the worse I felt.

'Why have all these experts who claim their methods work, never really helped?' 'Why was I getting worse?'

That's when I stumbled upon a book, to which I'm grateful for to this day. It was not what the book was about or the content of the book. But because the book gave me a realization which would change everything.

It was the book 'The Power of Positive Thinking' – by Norman Vincent Paele, and this was the realization:

'Right before you have a feeling, there's a thought. If you can hear those thoughts, you will become aware of your inner dialogue.

How you speak to yourself. And what's more important – most of these thoughts go unnoticed by people.'.

I connected the first dot.

My mind was somehow responsible for how I viewed myself and how I felt. So, after reading Vincent's book, I went on to practice the idea of monitoring my own thoughts.

Every time I went to work, I listened to what thoughts surfaced from my subconscious mind. Every time a colleague comes over, or I do something and feel anxious or stressed. I began to notice the inner dialogue I've never seen before.

I've seen my conscious thoughts before. What I should eat for dinner, or what happened this morning. But these were different. It was like a mental dialogue, that was going on deep inside my mind.

I thought the world was happening 'outside of me' and the actions I took were going to change how I feel about that world.

My whole world flipped in a moment.

I noticed the connection, of how my thoughts, were leading to feelings. Every time I failed, I blamed myself in my mind. Every time I was about to do something, self-doubt and blame kicked in. I was putting myself down to avoid doing things.

I began to see that it was my thoughts creating my experience. Thoughts I've never seen before. Which you can catch in a mere moment of them surfacing briefly, and then they're gone. That if you're not paying attention – *you'll miss them.*

Very soon after, I began to believe, that if my mind was responsible for why I am this way, and why I feel this way, and why other people see me the way I am – that if I could only change what I believe about myself, **It would all change.**

If I could only believe that I'm attractive, strong and confident – I would no longer see weakness. Instead of searching for guidance and books, I began to search for *'how could I change my beliefs?'.*

By that time, I've tried everything, from affirmations, to visualizations, to exercises or even personality tests. I even studied Advanced Psychology in University myself. But I never found a solution.

I never had my life consumed in such a way before. I never even saw myself that way before I got sick... But the autoimmune disease that I have developed made me feel pain on a daily basis.

It wasn't the world outside of me causing my experience. It was the world inside of my own mind which was creating my problems. It was the negative thoughts, which when repeated became habits – beliefs.

Think about it – you can have a confident person who has absolutely nothing, living in a trailer, drunk most of the time, with a stain on his shirt, yet experiencing joy, love and fulfillment. While on the other side, you can have a person who has a perfect family, all the money in the world, girls, success (from our point of view), yet he feels weak and vulnerable, that he needs more in order to arrive at a place where he can feel 'full'.

You see the difference is not in what they have in the outside world. The difference is what they have inside of their mind. How they see the world and how they see themselves. The meaning they place on things.

Let's take another example, which works even with animals. Let's say you find a puppy, who was abused by the previous owner. When you find him, he feels scared and threatened by you. Because you represent the same person that hurt him. You know he's hurting so you take him in, in order to help him heal.

At the beginning it's very hard, nothing you do seems to calm the puppy and make him feel the love that you feel. Eventually, in small steps, he begins to trust you. Eat the food, accept your touch and so on. Regardless of the fact that the puppy feels safe when you give him shelter, food and love (all the things he needs to survive) – he still can feel fear and avoid other people.

You see, it's not his fault what happened to him. But the incident became his memory. And his memory became a block between trusting, loving and putting himself out there into the world. It became a limitation.

He wants love, he wants to have friends, he wants to play, he wants to take the best food from a stranger – but he can't push past the barrier. Instead, he feels stress, anxiety, worry, hides behind you, and everything in his life feels unfulfilled. He would love to feel different, but he can't, because he has a belief and an association, which makes him see the world of potential pain. His survival begins to dictate how to feel (in our case also - how to think) and how to act/respond to different circumstances.

The real problem is not in the people, is not what happens outside of him, nor is it in what he does - it's in his belief about people.

From that belief he gets new beliefs, that taking food from strangers can mean pain, that approaching people can mean pain, that being himself can mean pain, that if he's not cautious can mean pain. Every future association about everything he does, comes from a different place.

We also come from an animal world, and pain works the same way with us. We avoid things, because we anticipate the worst-case scenario. **Pain.**

While this is an extreme example, we don't have to go far to notice this pattern all around us.

A girl who got her heart broken, putting barriers up. A guy trying to approach a girl, but feeling like he needs to get drunk – just so he doesn't feel the pain of losing her if he fails (or if he succeeds and loses her then). An anxious person putting up an ego (image) in order to be liked by other people, say and do all the right things, just to not feel the pain of being less than other people.

Every thought, feeling, word and action comes from a different place. Just because of how previous incidents or upbringing make us believe about the world and ourselves.

I came to realize that the reason why we don't notice how our experience is being created - is because we never look <u>inside of ourselves.</u>

From the moment we are born, we get told that the world is *'out there'*. Our parents teach us what means what, how the world works, what to do and not do.

But they never teach us to understand the processes going on inside our own minds and body. We never learn to become self-aware. To see how we think and feel and better yet - how it leads us into our experience in the real world.

To draw the connection between the two. To gain **balance.**

*'He who goes with his whole heart will get what he seeks. Only do not be of **Two Minds.**' - Reads the opening of a 1500-year-old Gospel 'The Lots of Mary.*

From the moment we meet other people, we share the same view of the world with them and only talk about the things happening outside of us.

We begin to live our lives always facing the outside world, looking at it, thinking about it, feeling what happens, and acting in response to how we are made to *feel.*

We never examine the process of how our body is creating our experience. Instead, we examine the world and how the world is creating our experience. We try to make sense of the world, what means what, if we did the right thing – and what should we do, in order to get what we want.

Every book we read teaches us methods, exercises, tips, tricks and secrets to do something outside of ourselves, in order to change how we feel. Like saying specific things; physically controlling our body language; wearing different clothes; acting before it's too late; faking it till you make it. Or to try and control the things we can't really take control of.

But have you ever noticed that the same advice that works for some people, doesn't work for others?

It's Not in What You Do. It's in The Place It's Coming From

When I began to see the pattern of how my thoughts were leading to my feelings, I noticed another pattern.

When I had negative self-talk and self-image, I was feeling anxious, self-conscious and stressed. Regardless of what I would say, it's like people could see 'where it's coming from'. Never giving any positive outcomes.

When you look at other people, say or do the same exact things – they get positive results.

Like the guru, being convinced that his thing works for him. He thinks differently, believes differently, feels different and when he does it – *it works*. So, he's convinced that it does. But when he teaches it to other people, other people can't seem to get the same results.

It's because peoples inside world doesn't reflect their actions on the outside. It doesn't appear authentic or congruent.

The difference is **not in what you do.**

In psychology it's a common understanding that people read people's sub-communication better than we read their words. That our language only makes up 7% of our communication.

For millions of years, we have communicated without words. Every time a person would come in with a smile, but his intention was to hurt you, you had to pick up his intention from seeing how he feels and what his body is communicating to you.

Communication helps us to survive.

Even today when a guy comes over to a girl with a pickup line, the moment she feels that he is using it in order to get something from her, and pretending, putting up false image just to get what he wants – *she feels negative emotions.* Like warning signals, that the communication is not genuine and not safe.

The worse the guy feels, the more the girl can pick up on it and feel repulsed by it. While other times, he can say it to a girl he finds less worried about missing out on – and it works.

When things work, he will go tell other guys to use this pick-up line. And it may not work for them. Just like the common self-help advice people give out. And it becomes a cycle of false perceptions of what works, passed on from people to people. Creating distraction and confusion in society, with people looking outside for that golden advice.

You see – the self is always coming through. Our sub communication is much more powerful than our words alone. People can pick up on how we feel and the place where we are coming from. That's why when we are anxious and have low self-worth, other people perceive us the same way, how we see ourselves.

They feel the place it's coming from, and we have that deep sense, that they might *see us*.

Every belief is powerful in such a way. Every idea of how you view yourself is how the world views you. Your place in the world is pre-determined by every belief creating your thoughts and feelings about yourself and the world.

When people believe their self-worth is limited, they can never surpass that limitation, no matter how hard they try.

People can try to get a promotion, just to find themselves that no one wants to give it to them. The problem is not the people, or the things we do. The problem is that we don't see how our minds and our beliefs create these barriers of pain which create our emotions communicating to the world.

The guy who wants to meet a beautiful girl, he doesn't know it's his past association of how painful it is to feel rejection, that makes him feel worried. Yet every time before approaching, he feels that the potential of the past experience can become realized once again. And his mind and body are trying to prevent him from potentially experiencing that pain.

His results resemble the total sum of everything he holds in his mind. Every barrier still stays as a barrier, every memory of pain still prevents him from getting what he wants.

It's called **conditioning.** Just like for any animal what means pain and what means pleasure. The same is in our society and our lives.

When you want the highest success at work, a promotion, success in business or have your relationship thrive, these invisible barriers live in our minds as beliefs and associations. They are interpretations of the world and ourselves, based on our past and *calibrated* by what we get from the 'outside world' – determining our self-image, possibilities and how we'll act.

I recommend reading that again.

We calibrate our lives based on the world outside of us, even when our minds are the ones creating our experience – already pre-determined by our held beliefs and memories of past experiences.

Mindset and how we see the world is the difference between people who people who are thriving in life and people who can't seem to get ahead. It's the projection of reality, that we get lost in. Without ever working on the projector itself.

You can find successful people openly talking about this subject, while being examples of their mindset and the success they were able to achieve. From actors like Denzel Washington, Jim Carrey, Jamie Fox, Will smith, Jennifer Lopez to singers like Ariana Grande, Lady Gaga, Beyonce, Bruno Mars, to influencers like Oprah Winfrey, Steve Harvey to fighters like Jon Jones, Muhammad Ali and Bruce Lee.

<u>By now it's no secret.</u> The power of the mind is well described in a book called 'The Secret' by Rhonda Byrne. Ever since Napoleon Hill, working under Thomas Edison instructions went on to study and examine the richest, wealthiest and most successful people in the world, after 20 years of research and work, he came back with one simple conclusion.

All success was created by the way they thought and saw the world. That's why he listed his discovery in one of the greatest Entrepreneurship books ever written 'Think and Grow Rich'.

However, the misinterpretation in both books and the idea of law of attraction/manifestation was that it is your thoughts that are the key to change. So, people went on to try and change their thinking, with methods of affirmations, visualization or meditation.

No one questioned – *what was creating those thoughts?* No one looked one step deeper, to understand that all thought is created – **by a belief.**

Because people who improved their thinking felt better, and because they felt it – it felt REAL.

Because their feelings fueled their belief in the method and the results it may bring – many people got out of the rut. While others continue to fail to get any results even today.

That conviction from people again got passed on, creating an ideal fantasy, that if you do exercises of thought (like affirmations & visualization), you will be able to manifest reality almost in a magical way.

Expensive cars, luxury, dream relationships will pop right into your life. And it appeals to everyone's desire to have their wishes come true.

But unfortunately, it's not our thoughts that create reality. It's our beliefs that give rise to perception and projection of the world we see – creating each thought, feeling, choice of word and action. Making us different, than the person next to us.

People afraid to put themselves out there, afraid of what other people will think of them, people are afraid to put their image on a dating website, and people can be afraid to approach another person just to say 'hi'. And there are people, who have instilled the highest level of mindset, to be able to achieve the impossible. Against all odds, what other people would say – *is impossible.*

The potential that is set in one's mind can override thousands of people with just intent, desire, or even opposition saying that you *'you won't make it'*.

When I found how to gain control of my beliefs inside my own mind - I got everything I always wanted. Like a cure, all my problems were solved. Within a matter of days, I went from feeling anxious and depressed to feeling strong and content, seeing other people approach me with respect and comfort. Like a 180-degree turnaround, *I got everything I could ever ask for.*

Because I changed my beliefs, with ease, I was able to meet the girl I would fall in love with, go from being broke and in debt to making $2k/day and have my business succeed. I became a consultant to businesses and individuals from companies like Apple, Google and Tesla. I became an Author and I'm able to live with joy of doing what I love, and see my expertise and practical method bring real, actual results to people all around the world.

Having an ability to control your mind, control your beliefs and in effect direct your thoughts, feelings and actions is one of the most powerful things you could ever have in your entire life.

Regardless of where you come from, or what you have right now – **you can have more.**

You can have what you want. And you can overcome any adverse situation creating barriers in your life.

How To Eliminate Pain, Fear & Invisible Barriers

One evening, back in 2016 my experience reached an unbearable moment.

It was a day after a night out, my hands were shaking, and in my head, I couldn't handle it anymore. After I became self-aware of my thinking, all I saw was negative thoughts, making me feel worse and worse.

That night I decided that it would be the last time I felt that way.

I came back home, took a herbal supplement to help me think, threw a notebook on my bed, sat down and said to myself *'I'm going to figure out **what is fear?**'*.

As I began to think, all the previous information I've gathered from the 100+ books I've read, top experts and their lessons suddenly began to connect.

I took an example of a spider, to have a more impersonal example. And I thought - you can be afraid of spiders, but if the spider isn't there – you can't feel fear.

It's only when the spider is there that causes fear, stress, anxiety or pain. It's only when the thing you BLEIEVE to be bad, can be experienced.

When the potential is there and when you do indeed experience that which you're afraid of, the feeling of fear appears like an emotion of **resistance**.

You want the spider to not be there. The body is saying to move away from it, so that you can survive.

Pain (fear) is an emotion of survival.

The closer you get, the bigger the feeling of resistance (fear). And the more you focus on it, the more you think about it, and the feelings begin to build up – *pushing you to move away from it.*

When I understood that fear gets built through resistance, I asked **'what is resistance then?'**. And very quickly I realized that resistance is simply <u>wanting for something to be different, than the way it is.</u>

The idea of resistance is an extremely powerful way of understanding pain and fear. Because we are led to believe that every emotion is <u>different</u>, that every feeling has a different name and meaning.

Feelings of *guilt, shame, embarrassment, humiliation, grief, anxiety* and so on.

But in reality, we are like any other animal, capable of feeling only two types of emotions – **pain and pleasure.**

These emotions are what move us. While pain pushes us, pleasure pulls us.

Different situations are simply themes that commonly re-occur. And when we create different labels for each theme – we confuse ourselves with what those <u>different</u> emotions mean.

So, when you first BELIEVE, that a spider can somehow hurt you, you <u>want for that not to happen</u>. And your mind automatically focuses on the negative belief, predicting the worst-case scenarios, building up resistance and pain to save you from what you believe may cause you pain.

Belief is what creates that resistance, from the mind creating our feelings. And because it appears that the outside thing is making us FEEL, we consider it coming from the real, physical world.

But in reality, it's a picked-up belief that a spider is somehow dangerous that is causing us to see the world that way.

It's not in the spider itself and it's not in the situation of the outside world. Because people who <u>believe</u> a spider is harmless – cannot experience any fear or resistance.

Which means that all fear, pain and even good emotions, can only be caused by our perception – **beliefs.**

It's your mind creating your experience. <u>It's your mind that creates your feelings.</u>

Secret Loophole: Source Of Negative Beliefs

This is probably one of the biggest secrets, that when people are unaware of, becomes very easy to fall into a cycle of negative thinking, self-image, lack, limitation – and even be controlled by.

And when you gain control of this principle, you can eliminate all that, and quite literally make your wishes come true.

After realizing how my experience was created, I went one step further and recalled a valuable lesson I've learned a while ago about how our brains work:

'The brain can't think in the past or in the future. It can think about the past or about the future. But every thought you have feeds back into the present moment. Your mind doesn't know time. Every thought you have, feeds back into the present.'

Based on this powerful principle, I've realized the source of all fear, pain and resistance in our lives. Notice how I've told you that wanting for something to be different, creates pain?

Well, the very idea of **'wanting'** feeds back into your mind, to the present moment – re-affirming, that you <u>don't have it in the moment.</u>

The way desire pushes us to get what we want is by making us see what we don't have. And it sounds pretty normal right?

You want to buy a car, you see yourself not having a car, you begin to notice how other people feel when they have a car, how cool it looks and feels when you do, you begin to imagine what it would be like if you had a car. Every thought shows you the difference from where you want to be, to where you are. Pushing you to work harder, save money and take necessary actions in order to buy a car. It's pretty cool and useful, there seems to be nothing wrong with 'desire', right?

Believing that it's painful to not own a car, will push you to get a car. The more pain you feel, the bigger the desire, the more you are pushed to buy the car faster.

The beauty of this principle and all human pain and suffering lies in the very idea I've mentioned in the earlier part – *'people believe the world is only out there'*. They don't really see the world inside, creating their lives.

So, what happens when you want something that comes from inside? What happens when you don't know how to get what you want?

<u>Things like self-confidence, self-esteem, courage, happiness, love, fulfillment, all of these things are qualities that can only come from within.</u>

If you believe you are confident, then you will feel, see yourself and act as a confident person. But when people want to be confident, their brain circles back into the present moment, showing them - that you're not confident right now. Making them feel, see themselves and act as someone who does not have confidence.

And because other people see them exactly how they see themselves, through how their body micro-communicates everything they say and do – the feelings within and the outside world re-affirms the very belief that they started with.

The desire will push them to read books, buy clothes, put makeup on, temporarily making them feel confident, of if they believe in these methods – they feel confidence only while they have that 'outside thing'. Believing it works. But then when they're all alone, by themselves, that self-belief of not being confident creeps right back in. When they move past that experience and take off their clothing or don't wear their makeup – the thoughts of self-doubt creep right back in, and they begin to see examples of 'not having it'.

While it may make sense in your mind with this confidence example, I want you to notice how examples of <u>this principle are all around you.</u>

When you consistently think about wanting something to be different, eventually it becomes a habit of thought – **a belief.**

Just like in grief after we lose someone, we begin to focus on wanting to hold on to them, just to see ourselves 24/7 that we don't have it, until we become depressed long-term...

Ever since Instagram came out, teenagers began to desire to look like their role-models, they began to desire to be like them. The more they wanted to be different, the worse they'd gotten. Depression and suicide rates became a vivid problem. It wasn't Instagram's fault; these are simply laws of nature that no expert is even aware of.

The same can go for a millionaire, wanting to feel fulfilled, believing that having money will give him what he desires. Every time he earns more money, he feels good temporarily, until he drifts back to realize 'he doesn't have it'.

When people see these examples, they begin to think that – money doesn't bring happiness. Yet you do have people who do feel fulfilled, and money does make their lives better. In reality it's not the money that is a problem – it's their conditioned beliefs, creating desires that can't be fulfilled by any amount of money.

In relationships, the honeymoon period hits when you finally get what you wanted - love. Both people give unconditionally, and you feel like you've finally found what you wanted, until people drift back into your beliefs and begin to see – not having it. They begin to desire it again. Soon enough, their minds begin to focus on how the partner is not making them feel loved. The relationship begins to drift apart, and they see how good it feels when they *'get it'* from the outside...

With divorce rates rising, cheating becoming an all-time high and fulfillment in relationships being an ever-present problem that people are trying to solve. Without much success, managing the outside things. Convincing one another, that a certain way of behaving works. And that you have to force yourself to behave differently, in order to feel it.

Financial situation, when people want money, only feeling pain every time, they swipe their credit card, ending up at the end of the month looking at their bank account, having the same feeling and same situation month in and month out.

Even people who understand their addictive behaviors and compulsion, they want things to be different than they are, but all they see is how they're not. And anything they do on the outside can't seem to get them out of the rat-race of the same experiences – in different circumstances. Each moment outside of their lives, appearing different than before.

You see the principles I lay out to you over here are nothing short of a miracle solution. All of them are acknowledged and supported by the science of Physiology and Psychology. <u>They are ever present.</u>

Principles are beyond powerful, because they are patterns that are always working. They have a reason behind – **why things work the way they work.**

When you acquire principles, and make use of them, you are ahead of everyone who is wandering in the wildlife of too much information, guessing and believing in what other people are convinced worked for them. That's the only way to make real, powerful transformation.

So, let's move toward the three powerful principles that you need in order to use your innate ability to change your beliefs and rewrite your subconscious mind.

And later I will share with you a couple of powerful principles that make this process work within days, without putting in much effort at all.

But just before we do, let me give you one more principle, that is the secret to all attainment and achievement of your desires. Because let's face it, you do have people who also want things outside of themselves, but can't seem to get what they want, right? And it would be pretty cool, to always be able to acquire what you dream of.

A Secret Place Where All Barriers Hide

People think that problems in their lives occur as a consequence of things happening outside.

Where In fact, we are creating and attracting those circumstances into our lives, based on every thought, feeling, action and decision we make.

Whether we see and take opportunities or are blinded by our minds and rationalize an excuse for them. All of this comes from our perspective.

I've worked on my career for 7 years straight without getting anywhere with my life, career and the success I wanted. Alongside that, I re-experienced the pain of losing my father at the age of 6, when me and my first girlfriend eventually still fell apart.

It was only after I've understood how beliefs work, that I got an opportunity to change the fate of my future relationships and my success.

You see we don't have just a few beliefs. We have an infinite number of beliefs and memories that guide our lives.

If you go back to the previous example of buying a car, it looks all good. If you want to buy a car, you'll find yourself pushed by your situation where you don't have one. Until you finally do get a car.

But what about all the people who think and believe they want a car but can't get one? What about all the people who want a relationship, and are pushed to go to bars, clubs and take on social events, yet still can't get what they want? What's the difference? What's the disconnect there?

Well, this is simply a conflict of beliefs. Beliefs are like a giant web. Millions of different beliefs and associations connect with each other inside our minds.

Think about it, what happens if you want to buy a car, but you have an association that not having money is painful?

Imagine you are growing up, and you grow up in poverty. You're just playing, but you hear your mother crying behind closed doors. Every time you go to the supermarket you want toys and candy, like your friends, but every time you ask your mom to buy them for you, you feel what she feels – the pain of not being able to.

Without much verbal explanation you can feel what she feels, and you can understand what those feelings mean. While you can't understand the situation, and why things are the way they are – you understand that it's painful not to have enough.

Now you grow up, you finish school and go straight to work. You get your money, life seems pretty cool. You can buy all the things you want for yourself, all the food you like, you can pay rent and even live alone. Throughout the time of growing up you get beliefs from the environment which make you desire to get a car, so you can look cooler, and maybe find a girlfriend. You can drive to places and see the world outside of the city. Maybe you even pick a model of the car you truly desire.

The more you think about it the more you want it. The more you walk on the streets the more you see that model everywhere. The more you want it the more you see how other people feel when they have it, going back home and realizing that you don't.

You must do something to get it. But every time you look at your bank account, you find yourself not having enough money to put aside. At the end of the month, you pay the rent, for necessities, and you find yourself that that car may be out of reach.

Without much awareness, both beliefs are true from the mind. 'I don't have money' and 'I don't have a car'. You don't see the barrier, the reason why, and you try to manage things outside of you, just to realize that you still can't seem to make it.

While this is again an obvious example, the same happens with relationships and people wanting love, but finding rejection painful. Wanting wealth but finding themselves spending themselves out. Wanting confidence but finding themselves not having it.

We have an infinite number of beliefs. And not all of them are created equal.

For example, everyone knows the common one **'fear of rejection'**. Most people are aware of it *(mostly in its literal form)*, because many people have it at a pretty high pain association level. And it can be felt everywhere.

If you look at people who have the biggest barriers and continue the rat-race of failed relationships, and difficulty of attaining them – are people who experienced a deep pain with losing someone when they were little. Or even if they didn't or don't remember – all it takes is for a baby to be hungry and cry, without any answer from a parent, for long enough, to where a baby begins to feel that he was left and abandoned. To where all his food, safety and shelter – his ability to survive is lost.

You see, all that it takes is to experience it. That experience becomes a memory, a belief of how painful something felt.

That pain creates a desire for the opposite, to want love and acceptance. The more you desire it, <u>the more you see you don't have it.</u>

And in the case of our spider/fear example – the closer you get to experiencing that potential of getting rejected, the more you are moved away from it. This is what makes want to have a fit body, but incapable of getting themselves to the gym. This is the source of all procrastination, barriers and excuses. We are internally made to find a way around it or choose the safe path – that leads us back to where we are.

The point is that when it comes to beliefs of association, beliefs like 'rejection' - **they are all around you.**

Whether you try to get a promotion, go and meet new people, put yourself out there, say the wrong thing, do the job bad, put the wrong picture on your Instagram, create a video and put yourself on camera, try to create your own business, try to make a sale, wear the wrong dress or anything else that society tells you, that it can bring about those consequences.

These are the invisible barriers that create unfulfillment, barriers of success, rat-race of escapism, rat-race of failed relationships and a ton of other issues we have no clear-cut solutions for.

On top of that, it actually leads people to realize their beliefs, to where they have the same experiences happen in different moments in time.

Now it's been a bit of a ride with me laying it out here in a short glimpse, just how powerful and influential your beliefs are in everything you call reality and everything you experience right now – and everything you will experience in the future.

Our beliefs are pre-determining what kind of lives we will have. A life of fulfilling and thriving relationships, or re-occurrence of past experiences disguised in new circumstances.

You see people who were lucky to have both parents in a joyous life and didn't experience much conditioning by the outside world have a laid-out path to a good life.

For those of us that did not have that, it is our responsibility to change how we feel about certain things and situations in life.

You can only take responsibility if you don't pass it on to the outside world, as being the cause of everything you are and everything you have.

And when you begin to look inside, you will find every obstacle and barrier, preventing you from having what you desire.

After the breakup, I took the responsibility to say that the pain I once felt when I lost my dad, will not influence my perceptions, thoughts, feelings, words and actions in the next relationship.

That I will recondition and neutralize that pain, to where it no longer has hold of my feelings, perceptions, thoughts, words and actions. And that I will remove all invisible barriers that are preventing me from getting actual results with my career and achieve the highest level of success that can be possible for me.

Today writing a book, creating a course, coaching people, reaching out to people, putting myself out there feels like a piece of cake to me. All the work I've done on my mind led me to find the exact lessons and principles of business that I was blind to before.

This is the only reason why I see constant results in my career. I can approach any person, girl or conversation with ease, and I am 1000% certain that I can feel good whether I have a person in my life or I don't. Because I always know there's no massive pain behind it. Relationships are effortless. Because you're always giving what you have, rather than trying to take, or see what you believe you don't have.

This is true freedom.

All of this makes life far easier and more fulfilling. Because in every area of life, whatever you do – you can be yourself. You can express yourself the way you are. There are no barriers to anything. This is true confidence and <u>courage</u>.

'Limits, like fears are often just an illusion.' – Michael Jordan

I'm seeing these same results in every student that undertakes the QPH method and puts in the effortless work to overtime his future the way he or she would wish it to be.

But these core beliefs, these associations that exist in everyday situations, everywhere – require knowledge and self-awareness to find.

In other words – **it's a process.**

As long as you understand the powerful ever-working principles that govern the power of your mind and your life – it's easy to achieve.

So, what is the QPH Method and what are these powerful principles? And how is it all backed by science already?

Let's cover the core principles of **how it all works.**

How to Control Thoughts, Emotions & Habits (On Demand)

Now I'm going to lay out the golden nugget bits of your new superpower, with which you'll be able to gain full control of your mind, reality and all associations that have been created on *autopilot*.

So, you can have choice and freedom in choosing your life, the way you want to see and live.

After understanding the first principle of how the brain works – that it can only function in the present moment, and that It creates beliefs that way - I've asked, *'how can I change a belief then?'*.

And found the first principle, which creates all change and transformation in the world.

This principle came from remembering a phrase once voiced by one of the guys online teaching men self-development – Owen Cook. After I asked that question, his words echoed in my mind:

'Everything in life is a paradox.'

The Secret Power of The Ying Yang Symbol

This is one of the most powerful laws of Physics and the universe, by which life works.

Whether you like it or not, it's always present, like gravity. You can't change it and you can't negate it. It's creating your life right this very moment, in everything you do.

The key in the case of changing beliefs and our lives is – how can you use it? But first, you have to really see it. Understand it. And begin to see it from within, so you can gain wisdom in how it's controlling your life each and every second.

It is the Universal Law of Polarity. Which states that everything has two sides. Everything moves from one side to another.

You have black and white, open and closed, voiced and unsaid. And one can does not exist without the other.

Without fear, you wouldn't know what love means. Without wrong you would know what is right. Without bad you wouldn't know what means good.

One always creates another. Like a Ying yang symbol, that existed for thousands of years, symbolizing transformation.

And inside you have dots, meaning that one always creates another. You cannot have a closed book and open at the same moment in time. But when you have a closed book, you can know the meaning of open.

The power of this principles lies in its definition – **you can't have both, at the same moment in time**.

When I've realized that 'wanting' for something to be different, than the way it is causes pain and discomfort, I considered applying the power of paradox to resistance.

But before, I wanted to simplify the very meaning of resistance into one word – which was 'wanting'. And asked myself how I was taught in school, what is an antonym (opposite) of the word 'wanting'?

And of course, it is – **_having_**.

And that's when it hit me. I wanted to have confidence, which I was always re-affirming that 'I don't have it'.

The more I was looking for a solution outside of myself, the more I couldn't find it. Because it can't come from the outside world. It can be influenced, somewhat, by your perception – if you believe something gives you confidence, then it will. But it can never last. Because the only things you carry with you are your beliefs and your perceptions about the world and yourself.

But if I was to look at how I already had the confidence, the same way, over time it would become a belief that I do indeed have confidence.

This is the power of gratitude which is listed in religion books from The Bible to Quran. It's the modern idea of self-improvement that gratitude is the all-powerful. That when you focus on what you have, you'll begin to have even more. And when you focus on wanting – _you'll never have enough._

All this time I was facing the wrong way. I realized that I was looking for something that can never be found, outside of me. That's why the more I looked, the more books I've read, the more I applied those external techniques – the more it led me to see that I don't have what I want.

And in order to begin to see confidence, instead of focusing on how to attain it, you have to focus on – how you already **have it.**

How The Cure is Also the Cause

Inside of your mind you have one of the most powerful mechanisms that create your reality.

This mechanism decides exactly what you will see and find in the world. And it is deeply connected to your subconscious mind and beliefs about yourself and the world.

It is located at the very base of your brain where it connects to the spinal cord. And it is your most powerful survival mechanism, which has to show you, and give you everything – *what you believe.*

It is called Reticular activation System. And it works like google, whatever belief is entered in the 'search bar', is the exact results that will be shown to you.

What it means in simple words is that when you want something you don't have, you re-affirm in your mind that at that moment, in-effect – *you do not have it.*

Your reticular activation system has to show you exactly what you believe in the real world. You begin to see examples, situations, events and perceptions from that exact angle.

The mechanism is not at fault for anything that you experience. It is there to show you the world, how you've learned it to be. It has to show you the world, you are familiar with. Because the only way you can survive in the world – is if you know how it works.

Because of this mechanism, millions of years ago we were able to recognize that if a tiger is running right at us, it means danger. And it doesn't matter if we find a goldmine of food and resources – we will run to survive.

Which highlights another principle – **pain is a stronger emotion.** It's an emotion of *survival*. And it will always overpower the emotion of pleasure. That's why people, when they can't let go of their negative circumstances, can't let go of what negative thoughts or feelings take over them. It begins to bother our lives, stop us from enjoying it, from fulfilling other areas of our lives like relationships, finances, career, self-development.

In today's world we don't have tigers and the danger, but we create painful associations with things, that do not cause us real danger. And they become our invisible barriers, that stop us or prevent us from moving to where we want to go.

Which leads us to another principle within the mind, that is trying to help us, but instead stops us from ever overcoming our pain, problems and achieving our desires, states and outcomes.

Why Poor get Poorer and Rich Get Richer

This principle defines the self-prison, that maintains our reality, the way it is. Only when you understand this principle you can escape the rat race and the struggle of any situation.

Inside of your mind you have your Rational Mind - another survival mechanism.

Because if you look at the previous mechanism there is a huge problem with it in terms of survival.

Imagine if you felt bad because you believed that it's your fault that the tiger ate your baby. Then all you would focus on, see and experience would be pain – overtaking every other emotion and experience.

How could you continue to live and survive?

Your body would begin to release cortisol, the stress hormone on constant basis, to where stress, anxiety and pain eventually would eat your body from inside-out. You would simply cease to exist, because of your own mind.

So, the first mechanism needs a counter-mechanism. Which explains why we have AND how Rational Mind works.

The Rational Mind has only one purpose – _to diffuse negative emotions_. To rationalize it, until your body is brought back into balance. To where pain is balanced by pleasure, and you are in a healthy state – right in the middle of the paradox. **Balanced.**

This is the beauty of god's creation. All elements of the human body are created with an exact balance of energy. That's why any medicine you take will always have some form of consequence, maybe not immediately, but absolutely indefinitely.

So, the way it works in our daily lives, is that the Rational Mind will kick into high gear every time we begin to go out-of-balance. When the pain rises – our mind will try to diffuse it. And it does so, by finding _pleasure_. Which often is disguised as a - **reason**.

There's two ways it can go.

We may want to go to the gym, but we feel like other people might see us, where pain overpowers the thing 'you should do'. So, we find a reason not to go _'It's Wednesday'_, _'Jack doesn't want to go with me, I don't like going alone'_ and so on.

Which becomes a new thought, and over time with enough emotion it becomes - <u>a new belief.</u>

And most of the time, when the sponsoring belief is of pain – the rationalized belief will be one that **doesn't serve us**. It will be thoughts and beliefs created – which will keep us in the same undesired condition, for as long as other beliefs allow us to be stuck in that place.

Only when other beliefs become more painful, that the one of 'not going to the gym', for example - not being able to find a partner, only then it can overpower those beliefs. And then that pain will push us past all the reasons falsely created, and we'll go to the gym.

The other way it can go is where we experience pain <u>coming from within</u> and can't find solutions on the 'outside'.

This type of pain and beliefs we carry everywhere we go. They are attached to our identity. And the way we rationalize that pain is by adjusting our self-image, blaming other people or taking actions and doing things that are pleasurable like drinking, smoking and eating unhealthily – just to find ourselves being exactly how we are. Or sometimes, even spiraling into a worse situation.

Again, until some other beliefs overpower our new reasons and beliefs, and we'll say 'enough is enough'. I have to get hold of my life and stop behaving this way.

But until then, people attempt to escape themselves for years – without ever changing their negative habits or doing things that are not in their favor. People come up with reasons for why world is the way that it is, for why Politicians are at fault, for why the Ex made me became the way I am, for why I became stronger and have risen my barriers in meeting people, for why I can't have success and why having money doesn't bring happiness.

<u>Everything is a reason to maintain one's beliefs.</u> And those reasons stem from each pain-based belief, that cannot get easily solved. *Especially by the outside world.*

This is the source and the reason why people are exactly where they are. And why others are able to keep growing without stopping. Why some people can't seem to make ends meet or get results in what they're doing. Or why sometimes it takes years and even decades. And why other people are finding it effortless to make more money, meet new people and have their relationships thrive and grow as they grow.

The matter of fact is that with the QPH Method you can change the entire course of your life. By changing and reconditioning the beliefs, the core-beliefs that got built without your conscious control and choice. And then every other belief on top begins to break and change on its own. Making you see new possibilities, opportunities and pumping different kinds of thoughts and feelings into your body and making you act toward an entirely different destination.

If you've ever read the book 'The Compound Effect' by Darren Hardy, you could easily understand that changing just 1 powerful belief, with the power of <u>time</u>, could change the entire destination of your life. And you could arrive in an entirely different place – *than you would've otherwise.*

I was hurt by the pain of losing my father; raised by a single mom working 3 jobs, to where at times of the great depression in the 90's she had to give away her food so that me and my sister could survive; I've never had enough money, seeing my friends buy crisps, and chocolates at school when I couldn't; I had the people closest to me saying that I should never dream about making big money; my relatives and my closest friends would have a laugh from me ever expressing that.

Briefly, for a short period, I lived within the boundaries of my mind, unable to see these invisible barriers, working for 7 years while being 8k in debt, bankrupt and owing 2k to my ex-girlfriend. <u>Without any results.</u>

And through the power of reconditioning the mind from all these invisible barriers, and pains, I was able to rise and build successful business, become an established Author, highest level expert in a new field, making 2k/day, and consulting highest level of people for sums that people can't earn even if they worked for 3 years straight.

If you'll notice, what I shared with you were all principles.

It is only a few out of a dozen principles that I collected over the years of developing this method. But each and every one of them is important for understanding what you're about to discover next.

Each and every principle can be explained – WHY things work the way they do. And as you can see, having an ability to understand and apply these principles to your life can bring you the greatest power and ability to get exactly what you want – and more.

So, now, how do we gain complete control over this process called life?

After realizing that I was facing the wrong way the first time, I now knew – instead of looking at how I want to have confidence, I had to see myself – **having it.**

I had to focus on the opposite, in order to create a new habit of thought.

How to Tap into the God Given Power

This is a principle as much as it is a function of your brain.

In fact, it is described within the Bible and Quran as the ultimate power, which was given to us by God himself.

A power that could draw energy from the very creator and fulfil one's deepest desires.

When I first came to realize how the first Principle of Life was dictating my experience, *I asked myself* – how can I control what I think about? How can I direct my focus?

In fact, the whole night I was sitting on my bed pioneering The QPH Method and looking for an ability to change my beliefs, all I did was *ask question after question.*

And again, because I've gathered information from over hundreds of books, one that immediately came into my mind was of Tony Robbins, where in his book 'Awaken the Gian Within', he highlights **the power of a question.**

'Every time you ask a question – you will get an answer. If you ask a better question, you will get a better answer.'.

I've realized - all I had to do was to **ask a question**, which will automatically imply – that 'I am confident'.

You just have to engineer that question, into giving you an answer to where the desired answer is already *implied*.

And it's very simple, when you ask a question, which measures your assumption, your mind can't help but look for examples, showing you – _HOW_ confident you already are?

In my mind I began to ask - *'How confident am I?'*.

With years of development of how to make this process faster and more effective, I've found that every word, and every detail of the question matters.

Early in the discovery phase of the method, I was lucky enough to naturally land on the presumption of the measure word HOW.

It's the most effective and most powerful way to focus on the estimate, and strength of a positive belief – making it grow stronger and stronger over time. Reaching the maximum level of confidence that you could have.

You see the power of question is directly linked to the power of beliefs.

The reason why all other methods like affirmations and visualization are not as effective is because they focus on *thoughts*.

Thoughts are something that come and go.

They are consequences of our beliefs and perceptions. And they can even arise from rationalizing our emotions, causing chaos and difficulty.

The biggest misconception in the self-development industry is that it is our thoughts that make up our world.

For thousands of years, from Philosophers to Great Authors who popularized the power of thought, Law of Attraction and Manifestation, like books Napoleon Hill 'Think and

Grow Rich' or Rhonda Byrne's 'The Secret' – they all focused on the power of thinking. On the energy created by *a single thought.*

But again, while dozens of people were inspired by the idea, and many fell to believe in its power – it distracted from where the real creation starts – **our beliefs.**

Think about it, every thought leads to an emotion. If you change from a negative thought to a positive one – you feel better. Because thoughts create our emotions.

So, when you fall for an idea, to change your thinking – you try it, and you do indeed feel better. You convince yourself further – that it's real, and it must work.

And I'm not going to lie, for many people that is enough to turn their lives around, and even lead their lives with this conviction (belief), emphasizing that it was the positive thinking or the Law of Attraction that led them to a better life.

But what about dozens of people who did the same exact things, affirmation and visualization, even in the same way but clearly didn't get the same results? Even now you can go online, just to find people each and every day attempting to 'manifest' a different life – without avail.

This is because a thought is a byproduct of a belief which produces thoughts on autopilot.

You have as many as 50,000 thoughts each day, 95% of which are the same thoughts as yesterday, repeating daily without your conscious choice. 20% of all your energy is going from your body, into your brain and is flowing through the pathways in your brain, that have been already laid out - like highways, creating your reality each and every second.

These highways of energy allow for energy to pass through quickly – it's the very mechanism, designed to show you your beliefs.

Each association guides your life so that you can react to the world around you and survive. These pathways are your beliefs, which dictate the entirety of your life. It is not individual thoughts that create your life, - it is how you see the world. What you have learned to associate pain and pleasure with. Like for any animal, guiding your feelings and behaviors. And as a consequence – _guiding our thinking_.

Your beliefs use the energy from your body, to create your thoughts, feelings and move you into action. The ultimate power of your mind therefore lies in your belief. And every belief gives birth to the next moment and experience in time. Showing you the very experience of life how you believe it to be.

This is actually the very mechanism of beliefs and how beliefs can be created. You see, beliefs produce experience.

And by the Law's of Life (Universal Law of Polarity) – <u>experience produces beliefs.</u>

Every time you see an experience that represents what you believe in, you say *'see I told you that's true'*. If you believe your boyfriend or girlfriend might be cheating, your mind through the RAS (Reticular Activation System) begins to show you experiences, where in fact it may appear true!

Experience then becomes a reference for the very belief that made you find that experience. Which explains the very power of a question.

'Ask and you shall receive.' Matthew (7:7)

'Call upon Me, I will answer you' – Quran verse 40:60

The Secret to Build Strong Beliefs

This is the most powerful principle to prove the power of your ability to gain control over your mind and what you get in life.

<u>Beliefs are built from energy (inside our bodies).</u>

In order for you to have a memory, you need to have an experience. That experience is felt through your experience of the world, giving you feelings and sensations. Which produces a memory.

And when something happens over and over again, the memory becomes so strong – **becoming a belief.**

Say you're sitting in a café and the kitchen gas pipe explodes. Maybe you don't get hurt but you see other people get hurt, and you feel the devastation they feel. Through your senses and experience of the outside world, this creates a lot of emotional energy in a single moment of time. Which easily builds a memory pathway in your brain.

If someone was to ask you *'what happened?!'*, you could recall it so easily. You could describe the conversation you were having, what you were eating, when, what and how it all happened. Even years later – you could recall that experience.

Beliefs need evidence. Because evidence creates experience, which generates emotion and energy inside of your body – to build beliefs.

That's why questions are so powerful – every time you ask a question, you get an answer – a reference which you see in your mind. And because thoughts and the act of seeing it creates a form of experience, it generates energy for a belief to be built.

When you ask a question 'how confident am I?' You begin to see examples, where in fact you did appear confident! As you see these reference examples in your mind, you feel the effects of you seeing it and thinking about it. Which makes it feel REAL.

This answer becomes a reference experience for building a new belief. The more you ask that question, the more different examples you see. The more important that outcome is for you – the more emotional it is. The more emotional you feel – the faster you build a belief.

But the power of a question doesn't stop there. Because you could almost call it – mystical.

Remember how I said, when people believe their partner might be cheating or say they don't love them anymore – people begin to see examples where in fact it feels real?

In Tony Robbins book he mentions a Psychology experiment, in which they tested the power of Focus.

They gathered a full room of people and they've asked the participants to find a certain type of colour *(say it was <u>blue</u>)* and count how many times they've found it in a room. And they gave plenty of time for this exercise.

After everyone has finished, the Psychologists now asked the participants to find a different type of colour and count how many times they've seen it in a room.

After that, they did something different. Now they've asked the participants to go back to the colour they were searching for the first time (<u>blue</u>), and look for it again, counting how many times they've seen it this time.

This is what they found.

When people have returned to the same colour, they found more of it, than they did the first time.

The problem is – there weren't more blue-coloured things, that appeared inside the room (as they had plenty of time to find them all the first time).

The Psychologists found and illustrated one powerful principle of focus (and the mind).

The participants began to identify anything that was close to blue – as blue. Even if it wasn't blue.

The conclusion Psychologists have made was that the brain is so powerful, that when you focus on finding something, it will find it – *even if it's not there.*

This is why people in relationships who experience jealousy can begin to see that their partner might be cheating on them, even if other person wouldn't see the same situation, the same way. And for the person – everything appears as potentially true, because 'he sees it'. It becomes his evidence.

This is the same reason why, after a honeymoon period when everything is going good in relationship – our belief of 'not being loved' begins to realize, and we begin to see how other person is falling short in giving that love, caring for us, doing things in relationship, and we begin to see only the negative things. We begin to see it more and more, rationalizing ourselves out of love.

While this principle of focus is extremely powerful in running our lives on autopilot – it's beyond powerful when you gain control over it.

Because it means that you can convince yourself and see absolutely anything. You can create whatever belief you want, even if doesn't make much sense to you in the moment. And even if it goes against your current beliefs.

This is where you can actually say that I found a God given ability from the bible itself. Ask and you shall receive is no longer a sounds good type of quote. It becomes a practical ability that we already have within us.

Yet nobody is using it the right way...

Not to worry, even if I am the first and only person teaching this and developing the method and understanding further, I will show you how there are no limits to what you can be, do or have. Only if you choose to take control of your mind, your beliefs and the process you call life.

But how can you not use it? When you ask a question, it doesn't even take 2 minutes to get an answer and find the reference experience. It's literally <u>effortless.</u>

When you begin to understand the power of this method, you can begin to see why I was able to make such a remarkable transformations with my life, why all my students preach The QPH method as somewhat of a Nobel Prize discovery and why dozens of people are actually able to make REAL transformation in their lives.

Unlike the idea of positive thinking, woo woo Law of Attraction hopeful thinking, affirmations or visualizations - all the transformations aren't just real, they are <u>permanent.</u>

Which leads us to the 3rd and final piece of the QPH Method.

As you can see the first principle revealed The Law of Polarity, represents the (P) letter in the method, the Question represents the (Q) letter in the method name.

Which leads us to...

How To Plant New Seeds in Your Mind

It may sound obvious. And it may sound easy to understand. Third – you need to build a habit.

But there's more to the Power of Habit than you may think. There's a reason why Albert Einstein called it the 8th wonder of the world.

The power of habit is something that is creating your life right this very moment, with every belief you hold in your mind. Not only dictating what you see and get in life – but how every bit of energy is slowly compounding into some form of outcome in your life.

Think about it, while you are the sum total of all your experiences in life, and all of your beliefs – the same way each individual belief inside, is building up into an outcome – outside of you.

It's like building a skill. You don't become a pro immediately. But if you do something over and over, the energy begins to compound, until you see yourself better than everyone else.

<u>So, a habit is simply repetition</u>. You have to ask that same question over and over, until it becomes a habit. Until it begins to roll on its own. Automatically creating reference experiences and showing you what you want to see in life.

As a matter of fact, Lets go back to the previous idea that you create beliefs from energy – have intense emotional experience (once). Because the second way your body uses energy to create memory and beliefs is – when you spend little energy, over and over.

For example, when you're learning how much is 5x5. It doesn't create much emotion; it's not thrilling or exciting.

So, you do it over and over again, until you create a new memory/belief.

Eventually that energy builds a new pathway inside your brain. Like every other habit, belief or association – it has its own pathway, a neuron (brain cell), through which energy travels effortlessly. Becoming a permanent belief.

And this is the cool part.

By The Law of Polarity, when a new belief begins to take place – the exact opposite belief <u>cannot exist.</u>

Which means when you are convinced that you are confident – *you cannot see yourself anything other than.*

When you believe you are confident, you cannot want to have confidence, because you already have it.

This is the power of the dynamic which is at play everywhere in the world. A person who has money doesn't worry about spending it. Because in his mind – he always has enough. A person who has love doesn't worry of losing a partner, because he always feels he is loved.

<u>You cannot see lack of something when you already have it.</u> And when you create a belief of having that which you want, you cannot have *lack, need, desire, compulsion or feel pain.*

People say everything comes in threes. That there's power behind this magical number. Well, this is the ultimate superpower of the three powerful principles in unity. Like the holy trinity, The QPH Method turns out to have the same.

When you will begin to create a habit, nothing else but a sure transformation will take place right in front of your eyes.

People who try different methods, tips, tricks, secrets, or practical applications in the outside world, cannot seem to make lasting change. In fact, people waste years and thousands upon thousands of dollars, in hopes that someone will help them achieve that.

When you go to counselling, or seek support, you can get a yearly subscription to a service which will merely make you feel better or change your perspective – without a complete and permanent fix. Like a band aid...

This is because most personal problems, including the problems in the outside world, come as an effect of our thoughts, words and actions produced by our minds and how we see the world. How we feel and move through the world.

Until you change your mind, specifically your beliefs – on a permanent basis, you will receive the same thoughts and feelings like the day before.

Which creates a life of illusion where you live each new moment in time, having the same experience in a different circumstance. *Making it appear **different.***

The Secret of Predicting the Future

The Law of Averages. It's a universal principle of Physics, which highlights the reason why we see the world outside of us so unpredictably. Uncapable of realizing that everything is coming from inside of us.

You see, nothing in life is stable. Energy is always moving. From one end to another, like the Law of Polarity says. Even the energy we measure through vibration goes up and down, or magnetic energy moves from pole to pole. The same is with our beliefs.

When we see the world, we don't see it stable. Our love for people goes up and down. Our sense of self and emotions go from good to bad on consistent basis.

The point is that by the power of beliefs – it always averages out to gives us exact average of who we are and what we believe (subconsciously) we deserve.

If you believe you lack confidence in life, you may in fact feel bad at times, rationalize and balance those bad emotions with good ones. Just to get back to feeling bad again once more. But on average, deep inside you are always exactly at the intensity of how you came to associate your self-belief.

If on a scale of 1-10 your self-belief is at 5, you will reach moments where you buy good clothing and surface beliefs will make you think that that clothing gives you confidence, rising to a 9. But when weakness hits and alcohol wears off you may as well fall into a 3.

As a consequence of your belief, you may miss some opportunities for a better job, arriving at a good enough place. After that you may lose that job and get a different job. But you see, regardless of these different experiences, your opportunities and what you end up holding on to in life – will be precisely exact what you subconsciously believe you deserve.

And not what you think you can have – but as a combination of all self-beliefs, beliefs about the world and associations of pain combined. In the end getting the exact reality that your mind dictates you deserve to have.

When people are unable to view the world inside of them and see how their experience is created, life seems unpredictable. Life seems to happen to us, rather than created from us. It becomes so easy to fall for this illusion and take reality as something separate from us. Passing away all responsibility and ability to change it. Which is what leaves people unable to find complete, clear-cut solutions to most of their problems and success in life.

When you do take all of these principles into account, you'll begin to see them all around you.

When you begin to practice self-awareness and self-discovery, facing inside – you will begin to see patterns of how these principles are always at play.

This awareness will give you belief in everything I'm sharing here with you. And this belief in the method and the process will give you the capability to gain control over each and every aspect of your life.

The first thing I ever did was to see where my feelings were really coming from. It was the observation of my deeper subconscious thoughts arising. Drawing the connection between my thoughts, perceptions and my experience. And then applying the QPH method, to make the changes, to those perceptions of the world.

This is the only way how you change those powerful, core-beliefs. This is how you discover your weak spots and barriers. This is how you begin to observe what you are getting in life and the experiences that are repeating. Questioning why are you feeling a certain way? Why is it repeating? What belief could this be coming from? What previous experience have I had, that could be linked to this one?

Because the matter of fact is that _you can't fix a problem without realizing there is one._

If you take responsibility, that it may in fact, come from inside of you – you have full control over it. If you pass responsibility that the world is the way that it is – you will continue to experience the world, the way that you believe it to be.

To this day I find it fascinating, that I was able to come out of depression in a matter of days without ever being able to become sad or depressed ever again. That I've changed the course of my life, pre-determined with a certain level of income and success. That I've reconditioned my childhood to where I can never feel pain while being in a relationship.

It was all a result of self-awareness combined with an ability to create powerful beliefs, that allowed me to find the problems – and then fix them completely.

You too can become limitless. But it's up to you to realize – is the life you're living right now your dream life? Is everything you have right now giving you deep fulfillment or is there something you would like to change?

The opportunity you have at this very moment hasn't existed ever before.

When you look around you, you'll see people's lives and thoughts on autopilot. The symptomatic world of too much information, distraction and self-conviction competing with one another of who has the answer.

You have an ability to make sure your life will never be the same and take complete ownership and full control over the future of your life and those who you will pass your experience to. Becoming a role model to the people around you and your future generations.

There's nothing more important to me than the future of my kids and the people that stand behind me. That's why I will always do everything in my power to help, serve and by on their side the best that I can be.

After learning all this information, remember this - **life is a choice**; you can choose to be a victim or anything else you'd like to be.

So how can you start and begin to choose the changes that you want to make, using The QPH Method?

Step 1: Apply the Law of Polarity

The most important part of the process is <u>knowing what you want.</u>

It's about what do you want to change and knowing the problem you want to solve.

<u>You can only do that if you're aware of your experience.</u> What thoughts are arising? What experiences are you getting? What undesirable conditions are repeating?

Apply the principles, read over them again and begin to see *'how they are being created in your life?'*.

This will require practice, because self-awareness is a skill. You have to become good at it, in order to be able to pinpoint the specifics of what is happening in your life, why it's happening and how you will change it.

Once you know what you want and how it's represented by your DESIRE, and how it's making you not have what you want, you can begin to turn it around.

For example, the first change I wanted to make was to have Confidence.

It was painful to not feel confident -> which made me want to have confidence -> which implied 'I'm not confident' to begin with -> which became a belief 'I'm not confident'.

I had to change that, and see that I am confident already.

This is how you think about beliefs which are **Identity based beliefs**. But you also have beliefs, which are **associations.**

For example, if you want to quit drinking, but you can't, it means you find it pleasurable, or it helps you escape the pain of let's say working a job. In this case it is an association – of it feeling good to have a drink.

If you want to change that you simply have to apply the Law of Polarity to begin to see – that it's painful to have a drink.

Remember, there's only two emotions you can associate something with. Feeling good (pleasure) or feeling bad (pain).

So, the first step is – find what you want, and change the association. Either from pain to pleasure or from believing you don't have something, into believing that you already have it.

I recommend you write it down as a statement, somewhere on a notepad or on your notes in your phone, so you can see it and hear how it sounds as a self-thought.

Step 2: Use the Power of a Question

The next step is you want to turn that statement or desire into a question which will imply how you already have it, or how you seek to find pain/pleasure in it.

For example, in the case of confidence, when it's painful to not feel confidence -> you want to have confidence -> which implies you're not confident.

To find examples that you are confident and see yourself that way, you can ask 'How confident am I?'.

When you begin to ask a question like that, your mind will begin to show you examples of how confident you appear in the situations you are in. You will begin to see your posture was upright, the way you handled yourself was good, the way you walked, the way you spoke – from a positive perspective.

When it comes to beliefs about the world and associations about different things – if you find it pleasurable to drink alcohol and you want to quit, you have to begin to see 'How **painful** does it feel when I drink alcohol?'.

As you begin to see that experience more and more painful, you will naturally see yourself move away from it. You won't even have to try and resist.

You can create motivation, stop addictive habits and change the way you see things outside of yourself.

When you know what you want, it becomes very easy to do. You just take a notebook or notes on your phone and write down this final question, as a question you can remind yourself to ask yourself consistently. It will take mere seconds to do, and you'll begin to gather reference examples for a new belief to become true.

However, there's a principle within the method that you **cannot miss**.

The power of the question doesn't lie in asking it. When you ask a question, it has absolute zero value. You have to get an answer from your own mind.

Remember 'Ask and you shall receive'. The value is not in asking, but it's in receiving. So, every time you ask a question within your own mind it's imperative that you get an answer. Because that answer becomes a reference for a new belief.

Sometimes, you may not notice it, sometimes you may be too tired. Simply ask that question one more time, until you do get an answer. And every time you do, with each day it will become easier and easier.

There's a short timeframe right after asking a question, during which your mind will find what you seek. The key is not rushing into the next question or to get distracted by life.

This is a crucial principle, which can determine success and failure in creating a new belief.

The power however lies in that when you do create a belief once, you will never have to do this ever again. Your mind will begin to show you that which you look for **on autopilot.**

It's well worth the investment, in spite of the little time it takes.

Step 3: Use the Power of Habit

As you can see The QPH Method is very simple and easy to do. But like every paradox – it's also easy not to do.

For most people change is hard. People are distracted by the life outside of us. We are busy with responding to things happening outside. And when we have to do anything practical, it becomes an effort people do not want to make.

Especially if it takes time or you have to do it over and over for it to work.

That's why most step-by-step programs, workbooks, diaries, exercises make it so easy for people to drop at any point in life, never to pick it up again.

The good news is that while you can do this whole method inside your mind without ever doing any work or writing things out – you can also make it entirely _effortless._

Before I reveal to you the powerful method of how to apply The QPH Method in your life, let's quickly cover the debate – _how long does it take to create a new habit?_

If you look around, different experts argue for different timeframes. Some people say it takes 21 days, others say it takes 30 days and some scientific research even says that it takes 66 days. So, when you want to make a change in your mind – how long should you repeat asking the question for?

This is where practice and theory set apart. You see in scientific research on paper it's very easy to assume that because it's scientifically conducted research, that it's the correct number. However, it becomes more complicated when you question what kind of habit was being built over there and with what method? What if other people had opposing feelings and associations to the habit being built, and researchers simply took an average of all people tested?

The first time I've applied The QPH Method I didn't have much doubt. Because I've found that most people who actually work in a practical way with the mind, such as world class Hypnotherapists, who could achieve those transformations within the mind – they believed 21 days is enough, if it's done correctly. While other experts who work with the mind and the functions of the brain estimate around 30 days to be certain.

This is how I drew a simple conclusion, in the same way that I saw it. 21 days is enough, but I would rather resolve to ask the question for **30** days, just to be make sure. Because if you put things to perspective, I will spend 2 out of my day (actually far less), for **30** days in order to gain what I want – for the rest of my life. I have always seen this as more than a worthy investment. And that's how I've always practiced this method. It never failed. Neither did any of the people who used it the same way.

You see the power of this method lies in its ability to create a reference inside your mind. A perceived experience. Which by how the mind works – thought always produces and emotion. And emotion is biological energy used to build and rebuild our bodies, to create energy.

So, if you do ask a question every single day, for **30** days, there's no way it cannot work. Eventually you build a new pathway within the brain, which begins to allow for energy to pass through automatically. The same way how you see reality right this very minute.

In other words, The QPH Method is not only backed by the Principles of Psychology, Physics and Biology, but – it's bulletproof.

And from my experience with teaching people how to use it – the results speak for themselves.

The Crucial Application Method

Indeed, if you choose only one change, only one transformation – you can simply put all of your effort into asking that question as much as you can in the privacy of your own mind.

And if you have a strong desire for the outcome you wish, it will carry you through – helping you remember to ask that question.

I call this method *The Crucial Application method.*

Because when you really need to come out of the dark, it is the most powerful way to do it. Your desire carries you through the effort. You'll ask the question relentlessly. Because you do it often, you'll build a habit where your mind begins to seek far more reference examples at a far greater rate than if you would just ask that question once.

Once it becomes a habit – it will continue running in the back of your mind at the same rate. Meaning you will get what you desire, reaping a far bigger reward.

That's how I've done it the first time and went from depressive to feeling totally confident within day. The transformation was **immensely powerful and fast.**

After my first relationship failed, and my career was non-existent, I've realized that there's more work to be done in order to unbind other invisible barriers and experiences of my life.

What I did was pick back up The QPH Method and I knew I had to do a lot more than just ask one question and leave it behind.

So let me share with you how you can begin to reshape multiple aspects of your life at once, without putting in much effort at all, how you can remember to use The QPH Method and still make a strong transformation of your beliefs.

Easy Method to Reprogram Your Mind

One of the most powerful things in human transformation is to be able to get what you want, without limitation.

To spark your fingers, and be able to accomplish things, achieve your dreams and reach your desired destination.

You can only accomplish this when you know what changes to make. This is why <u>self-discovery</u> and <u>education</u> is your best bet at reaching a point in your life where you are rapidly shaping life into the life you desire to live.

When you understand the processes and principles at play, what association has what consequences, you may then have more work to be done, than just ask one question or change one belief.

When I broke up with my first girlfriend, I realized there's more work to be done both for the quality of my relationships and for the success of my future.

After I've learned a broader perspective of how different conditions get created, I needed a tool so that I could recondition my mind of past experiences. Meaning asking many different questions, changing different types of beliefs and associations from different angles.

You have to make it make it more practical, so that it doesn't interfere with life, take up any time and still works as powerfully as the method by itself.

There was one really cool way to achieve this - leverage the workings of your mind. How do you do this?

There's a special function of how your mind always works. <u>Your mind never rests.</u> It's in constant motion transmitting energy from your body, through your mind creating thoughts, feelings and actions every single second while you are awake – *and while you're sleeping.*

Every thought you have produces a feeling. That feeling leads you into an experience. Where that experience feeds back into your body and creates a new thought.

Have you ever noticed when you think about something, say something happened your friend left you in abrupt way - you felt bad about it, you begin to think about it, and spiral into compulsively thinking about it? The thoughts create your feelings creating new thoughts, that continue to roll. Often even if you stuff them away, they keep coming back.

If you think about it and focus on it, the energy compounds until you can't take anymore, and the feelings push you to action – you call your friend to find out what was wrong.

The same happens after breakups, conflicts, fights and even falling for someone. Whether it's negative or positive. The rational mind takes over to find reasons for the experience.

What I've found is that you can leverage these processes of your mind to get more out of The QPH Method, while doing less.

Because once you set your mind in motion – it works on autopilot, creating reference experiences while you sleep.

This is why this method by comparison is far easier and more effective than any other workbook, system, exercise you can undertake.

Our minds are creative, visual. When you go to sleep it loses sense of reality...

The boundaries of the seen and heard fade. You become free to create the same experiences and emotions without limits.

That's why dreams often represent what we already hold in our minds, and often predict what reality may fall into our lives, in our future producing a sense of a **Deja vu.**

And because thoughts, feelings and experiences always lead to a new thought, you can set your mind in motion, directing in which way it will <u>continue to go</u> and what the mind will <u>continue to think about.</u>

You can leverage this simply by reading the questions in your notes, as:

1. The last thing right before bed, and

2. The first thing upon waking.

As you do that, if you can recall your dreams, you'll often find that your dreams are relative to the direction you set your mind in motion to. And when you do it in the morning – throughout the day, examples and references pop back into your mind. As if subconsciously, *still asking the very same question.*

On top of that, these are the times when the body preserves the energy to run to the vital organs and the brain for a reset. Allocating more energy and leveraging the very creation of <u>new beliefs.</u>

And this way you can read a multitude of questions all in one go, and easily associate this exercise with a daily routine – as being the last thing you do before you put your phone down. Saying to yourself *'I have to ask questions before I set the alarm and sleep'.* And the first thing you do when you wake up, before you start your day.

When you do it for the first time, for 30 days, creating another habit, of always consciously creating changes you wish to have in your life.

Often reading 20-30 questions won't even take you 2 minutes. But again, it will all depend on your knowledge and wisdom of how your life, you call reality, is being created through your mind.

The next steps to take will therefore depend on your life and your situation. Because I've found that I can never make people change, or better yet do what they don't want. It's all about your situation in your life and the perspective of how badly you want to have a difference in your life.

How To Predictably Change Your Fate

Are you aware how powerful of an opportunity you have? Let me illustrate the new power you now can hold in your hands.

There was once a boy who dreamed of becoming a professional basketball player. He started playing basketball when he was 3.

When he was 12 years old, he went to Philadelphia's basketball league where his father and uncle once played and were all-time great basketball players. He was thrilled to be able to follow in the footsteps of his father.

For the entire summer while playing in the Sonny Hill Future League, he didn't score one point. Not a free throw, not an accidental layup, not even a lucky ball.

He compared himself to his father and uncle at the top of the league legends list, feeling ashamed – he sat on the side crying. And then his father walked up, hugged him and said, *'whether you score 0 or you score 60, I'm going to love you no matter what.'*.

Many years later Kobe Bryant became one of the greatest players who ever played the game, as one of the most memorable legends in NBA history. After retirement he said – 'That is the most important thing you can say to a child'.

You see, while for many people that may seem like a natural occurrence, one of the biggest fear-based beliefs we all hold as a natural association in our minds is a fear of rejection. A fear that if our parents leave, we may not have food, shelter or the ability to survive.

It is the first belief and the first association we create as children. What his father did at that moment changed that association into total and unconditional love and acceptance. In other words, there was nothing wrong he could do, in order to lose it.

This is what allowed him to push himself in the face of adversity. In moments where people can turn against you. Where you can lose your close ones. Where all the cameras are directed at you. And when everything is on the line.

He was unafraid. With zero resistance to the present moment.

Because it's a core belief, from which all other beliefs stem, everything he did and all the opportunities he sought out were open to him.

He was even fearless to approach the best basketball player in history Michael Jordan, play against him as an opponent and then ask for advice to teach him. Something most people wouldn't have the guts to do, trying to protect their ego and self-image.

If you ever observed him as a person, in comparison to other people, he had a sense of calmness. He left his career with certainty and calmness. He always seemed authentic, contempt and unswayed by circumstances around him. When opponents would try to break him or say something to him, he never got triggered, he never had to react or defend himself compulsively.

You see when you hold these powerful beliefs – they do not change who you are. You don't appear different like some superhero. You are simply moving through life having more <u>balance</u> and <u>self-sufficiency.</u>

Like Bruce Lee said, something that is extremely hard to achieve even for someone like him – is being authentic and expressing oneself honestly, through balance, with harmony, without being affected by the ego or the outside world.

Regardless of sports, you also have people with fortunate upbringing who have the highest quality relationships, thrive in the world of business, live each day with passion and fulfillment and have little to no barriers to getting what they want.

I had the same luxury, for nearly 25 years of my life to live and grow on the other side of conformity, mediocrity and a life given to me. But with this knowledge and powerful ability to recondition and rewrite the past I'm able to experience what it means to live a life on the other side - where invisible barriers don't hold you back.

If I hadn't taken a decision, to consciously take control of my fate, and direct it on my own accord, right now I would be a personal trainer, trying to make it. My relationship would slowly but surely follow the same route where eventually my feelings and behaviors would pull us apart. I would be living from paycheck to paycheck, every time I swipe my credit card at a supermarket feeling a moment of pain... At the end of the month looking at an ever-lasting overdraft...

As I'm writing this, all of this is familiar to me. Because I was there. And I can't describe to you the feeling I feel when I know that I can never go back. Because I made myself that way.

There is nothing more powerful than your ability to change your fate. Every feeling you feel, and every action you take.

Even if your life isn't that bad, it's easy. Ask yourself – is there something really great about it? Are you making it the best it could be? Are you living the greatest life you could be living?

Notice where you are right now and where your life is going. And if you keep heading the same direction, where will you be in 5 years? 10 years?

If you don't feel like it's as great as you wish it to be, realize that you have an opportunity to change it here and now. Every belief is like a seed, that is growing over time. Creating the sum total of everything you call life. And the sooner you plant the right seeds, the sooner they will blossom.

Up until this moment, you were growing seeds inside your mind that were given to you. You did not consciously choose the experiences you will have ahead of time. Neither you did after you were born. The same way I didn't choose how I will feel and be affected by losing my father at the age of 6.

Things happen to us. And things that happen to us – shape us.

After discovering The QPH Method, **you have a choice.**

So, <u>what are you going to do?</u>

If you've enjoyed this book, please consider leaving a positive review and let us know how valuable you found this book.

All the best,

Vytas Kas.

About The Author

Vytas Kas is an established Author, Professional Consultant, Pioneer and developer of The QPH Method - a new human ability to change human beliefs and associations within the subconscious mind.

He is world's leading expert, specializing in human mind and belief reprogramming, through practical methodology and principles.

His work greatly contributes to the Science of Psychology, Philosophy, Business & Marketing and Medical Sciences. In 2015, University of Aberdeen, Scotland, Vytas was awarded with a diploma in Sports Medicine, in which he studied Advanced Psychology, Medical Sciences and Coaching.

Vytas findings provide a practical method for Psychologists and Practitioners all over the world, to effectively deal with psychological transformation.

He is a mentor and a hero to people who suffer from Psychologically induced mental health conditions, procrastination, relationship problems, personal barriers, trauma, negative self-image, anxiety and other problems affecting one's personal quality of life, experience and achievement.

For more, please visit vytas-kas.com.

Recommended Resources for Further Development:

Self-Master Academy - The only place where you can self-educate, master your ability to change beliefs, and receive help and support. Discover different beliefs and their impact in your life, so you can gain conscious control of your life, strengthen your confidence, build courage, improve your relationships and achieve your dream life faster than ever before.

✓ **Core-Beliefs & Their Reconditioning**

✓ **Discovery of Most Powerful & Impactful Beliefs**

✓ **How to Accelerate Belief Transformation**

✓ **Energy Flow Beliefs (7 Chakra's)**

✓ **Valuable Resources**

✓ **Ask Questions & Get Support**

Join the vast community of Freedom Academy, people who are transforming their lives by reprogramming their beliefs.

For more please visit *selfmasteracademy.com*

Recommended Reading:

The QPH Method: Gain Control of Your Beliefs, Emotions & Success in Life – at The Speed of Thought

(Full Book, by Vytas Kas)

amazon   BARNES&NOBLE   Apple Books.   Rakuten kobo   bibliotheca